P9-CAO-462

7
TRUTHS FROM EXPERIENCING
GOD

To:

From:

"*God's activity is far greater than anything we could aspire to do for Him.*"

– Henry Blackaby

© 2007 LifeWay Press®

Second printing July 2008

ISBN 978-1-4158-6513-2
Item 005127384

Dewey decimal classification: 231
Subject heading: GOD—WILL

Cover art: Mike Wimmer is one of the nation's leading illustrators. He has done numerous book covers, movie posters, and images used in major national advertising campaigns. When he was asked to paint the portrait of Moses for *Experiencing God,* Mike's extensive research, talent, and commitment led to a classic rendition of the prophet's experience with God at the burning bush.

Unless indicated otherwise, Scripture quotations are from the Holy Bible, New International Version, copyright © 1973, 1978, 1984 by International Bible Society. Scripture quotations marked NKJV are from the New King James Version. Copyright © 1979, 1980, 1982, Thomas Nelson, Inc., Publishers.

To order additional copies of this resource, write to LifeWay Church Resources Customer Service; One LifeWay Plaza; Nashville, TN 37234-0113; e-mail orderentry@lifeway.com; fax (615) 251-5933; phone toll free (800) 458-2772; order online at www.lifeway.com; or visit the LifeWay Christian Store serving you.

Printed in the United States of America

Leadership and Adult Publishing
LifeWay Church Resources
One LifeWay Plaza
Nashville, TN 37234-0175

TRUTH 1:
GOD IS AT WORK AROUND YOU

God Knows Who You Are

At the end of the first chapter of the Gospel of John, there is a wonderful moment in the life of Nathanael, a soon-to-be disciple of Jesus, when Jesus chooses him as a disciple. As Nathanael was brought to meet Jesus, Jesus let Nathanael know that He already knew him. In John 1:48, Nathanael asked, "How do you know me?"

Isn't that an amazing question for someone talking to God! Do you think that God knows you? He has known you since before you could even know that He knows you!

Nathanael said to Jesus, "Rabbi, you are the Son of God; you are the King of Israel."

Jesus said, "You believe because I told you I saw you under the fig tree. You shall see greater things than that" (John 1:49-50).

A church I pastored began to sense God leading us to an outreach ministry to the university campus. Neither I nor our church had done student work before. Our denominational student-ministries department recommended we begin with a Bible study in the dormitories. For more than a year we tried to start one, but we were unsuccessful.

One Sunday I pulled our students together and said, "This week I want you to go to the campus, watch to see where God is working, and join Him." They asked me to explain. God had impressed on my heart these two Scriptures:

"There is no one righteous, not even one; there is no one who understands, no one who seeks God" (Romans 3:10-11).

"No one can come to me [Jesus] unless the Father who sent me draws him" (John 6:44).

I explained, "According to these passages, people don't seek God on their own initiative. They won't ask about spiritual matters unless God is working in their lives. When you encounter someone who is seeking God or asking about spiritual matters, you are seeing God at work."

I also told our students, "If someone asks you spiritual questions, whatever else you have scheduled, cancel your plans. Go with that individual and look to see what God is doing in that person's life." That week our students went out to see where God was at work on their campus and to join Him.

On Wednesday one of the young women reported, "Pastor, a girl who has been in classes with me for almost two years came to me after class today. She said, 'I think you might be a Christian. I need to talk to you.' I remembered what you said. I had a class at that time, but I skipped it. We went to the cafeteria to talk. She said, 'Eleven of us girls have been studying the Bible, and none of us are Christians. Do you know someone who can lead us in a Bible study?'"

As a result of that contact, we started three Bible-study groups in the women's dorms and two in the men's dorm. For two years we had tried to do something for God and failed. For three days we looked to see where God was working and joined Him. What a difference that made!

A God-Centered Plan Is God's Plan

Many people are familiar with the story of Noah who built an ark to escape the flood. Noah was willing to serve God. Neither he nor anyone else had heard of a catastrophic flood like the one for which God told Noah to prepare. What about any of Noah's plans to serve God? They would not make much sense in light of the coming destruction, would they? Noah was not calling God in to help him accomplish what he was dreaming of doing for God.

God never asks people to dream up something to do for Him. We do not sit and dream about what we want to do for God and then call God in to help us accomplish it.

The pattern in Scripture is that we submit ourselves to God. Then we wait until God shows us what He is about to do, or we watch to see what God is already doing around us and join Him.

From Death Row to Life Row

God-centered living always affects others' lives. Being certain God is always at work around you will affect your relationships with other people.

When Karla Faye Tucker was on death row in the Gatesville Women's Prison in Texas, she became a Christian. Some faithful Christians led her through the book *Experiencing God*. Her life was so changed that she began to teach other inmates on death row. Many of the women came to know Jesus as Savior and embraced true life in Christ. Because of this, they renamed death row to "Life Row." Eventually, Karla was executed for her crime, but her testimony affected a nation and touched a world.

God Is at Work Around You

To live a God-centered life, you must focus your life on God's purposes and not on your own plans. You must seek God's perspective in your circumstances rather than your own distorted human outlook. When God starts to do something in the world, He takes the initiative to reveal His will to people. For some divine reason He has chosen to involve His people in accomplishing His purposes.

Understanding what God is about to do where you are is more important than telling God what you want to do for Him. What good would it have done for Abraham to tell God about his plans to take a survey of Sodom and Gomorrah and go door-to-door witnessing the day after God was going to destroy the cities? What good would you do by making long-range plans in your church if God brings judgment on your nation or your church before you implement them?

You need to know what God has on His agenda for your church, community, and nation at this time in history. Then, you and your church can adjust your lives to God so He can move you into the mainstream of His activity. Though God will not give you a detailed schedule, He will let you know one step at a time how you and your church need to respond to what He is doing.

We adjust our lives to God so He will do through us what He wants to accomplish. God is not our servant, who needs to adjust His activity to fit into our plans. We are His servants, and we adjust our lives to what He is about to do. If we do not submit, God will allow us to follow our own devices. In following them, however, we will never experience what God wanted to do on our behalf or through us for others.

Remember, God is at work around you.

NOTES

TRUTH 2:
GOD PURSUES A LOVE RELATIONSHIP WITH YOU

God Forever Convinced Me that He Loved Me

When our only daughter Carrie was 16, the doctors told us she had an advanced case of cancer. We had to take her through chemotherapy and radiation. We suffered along with Carrie as we watched her experience the severe sickness that accompanies the treatments. Some people face such an experience by blaming God and questioning why He doesn't love them anymore. Carrie's cancer treatments could have been a devastating experience for us. Did God still love us? Yes. Had His love changed? No, He still cared for us with an infinite love.

When you face circumstances like this, you can ask God to explain what is happening. We did that. We asked Him what we should do. I raised all of those questions, but I never said, "Lord, I guess You don't love me."

Long before this experience with Carrie, I had made a determination: no matter what my circumstances, I would only look at my situation against the backdrop of the cross. In the death and resurrection of Jesus Christ, God forever convinced me that He loved me. For this reason, during Carrie's illness, I could go before the Heavenly Father and see behind my daughter the cross of Jesus Christ. I said, "Father, don't ever let me look at my life and question Your love for me. Your love for me was settled on the cross. That has never changed and will never change." Our love relationship with the Heavenly Father sustained us through an extremely difficult time.

Are You Running from Love?

Because of love, there is no depth to which you can go that the grace of God will not go further still. There is no extent to which sin can get a hold of your life that the immensity of His salvation will not extend beyond the sin to keep it from overtaking you. There is no sin in your life that is causing you to stumble for which God has not more than adequately provided a solution.

I was in Arkansas leading a conference. After the conference, a man came up to me and said, "Henry, I didn't want to be here tonight." He was a married man with older children. Yet there he was, standing before me, tears streaming down his face, ready to tell me what had brought him to this point in his life.

He said, "I have a hard heart. I was in Vietnam and saw such brokenness and hurt that my heart became hard. I turned to alcohol and all kinds of stuff."

And he said, "My heart is so hard tonight that I am about to lose my wife, lose my children, and my job." He looked right at me and said, "It's about to kill me. Do you know anything that can help me?"

"Why," I said, "I do indeed."

I turned with him to Ezekiel 36:25-26 and asked him to read it to me.

"I will sprinkle clean water on you, and you will be clean; I will cleanse you from all your impurities and from all your idols. I will give you a new heart and put a new spirit in you; I will remove from you your heart of stone and give you a heart of flesh. And I will put my Spirit in you and move you to follow my decrees and be careful to keep my laws."

I asked, "Do you believe that the God who said this loves you and will make a new heart for you out of your stony heart?" He said, "Yes." I asked, "Would you like me to pray with you?" Again, he said, "Yes." So I prayed, "Oh Lord, You put this Scripture here for this dear brother. Would You, right now, come into his heart and read his heart? He wants a stony heart removed as much as anyone I have ever seen. Lord, would you come and do what You promised?" I looked up, and with more tears streaming down his cheeks, the man said, "It's gone! It's gone! My stony heart isn't there anymore!"

Now this man is serving God. He has become a nurse and a writer for inspirational magazines. I saw him again at a conference a few years later. This time, a handsome young man was standing beside him. Turning to me, the man said, "Henry, I just wanted my son to know the man God used to help his daddy get rid of his hard heart."

Love Leads to Reconciliation

Scripture indicates that God has a heart for reconciliation. It is so important to God that He said we should be reconciled with anyone who has something against us (Matthew 5:23-24). Yet, God knows how difficult it is to be reconciled with people and how difficult it is to get them to love us in return. God sent prophets, gave us the Old Testament, and finally sent His only Son. People rejected all of God's efforts and even crucified His only Son. But God continues to reach out to us. We can experience His salvation because He has done what it takes for us to be reconciled with Him.

How do we join Him in His work? Paul said that God has given us the "ministry of reconciliation" (2 Corinthians 5:18). That is, having experienced first-hand God's reconciliation with us, we are now His ambassadors, helping others experience reconciliation with God the same way we have; letting God show them His love through us.

The question may be asked, what if people don't respond to our attempts to be reconciled with them? Did you respond to God the first time He sought to be reconciled with you? Yet, God continues to reach out to humanity out of His grace because He loves us.

Final, Total, and Complete

No matter what your circumstances are, God's love never changes. The cross, the death of Jesus Christ, and His resurrection are God's final, total, and complete expression of His love for you. Never allow your heart to question God's love. Settle it on the front end of your desire to know Him and experience Him. He loves you. He created you for a love relationship. He has been pursuing you in that love relationship. Every encounter He has with you is an expression of His love for you. God would cease to be God if He expressed Himself in any way other than perfect love!

God takes the initiative to bring you into a deeply personal relationship. He created you for fellowship with Himself. That is the purpose of your life. This love relationship can and should be real and personal to you.

TRUTH 3:
GOD INVITES YOU TO JOIN HIM

God Is the Provider

When the church I led in Canada started its first mission, we called Jack Conner as our mission pastor. However, we had no money for moving expenses and no funds for his salary. Jack had three children in school, so we felt we ought to pay him at least a modest salary to provide for his family. We prayed that God would provide for his moving expenses and salary. I had never guided a church to do that before. We stepped out in faith, believing God wanted Jack to pastor our mission in Prince Albert. Except for a few people in California, I didn't know anyone who could help us financially.

I began to ask myself how God might ever make this provision. Then it dawned on me that as long as God knew where I was, He could cause anyone in the world to know where I was. As long as He knew our situation, He could place our need on the heart of anyone He chose.

Jack started his move of faith to Canada, convinced that God had called him. I then received a letter from a church in Fayetteville, Arkansas, that read, "God has laid it on our heart to send one percent of our mission giving to Saskatchewan missions. We are sending a check to use however you choose." I did not know how they got involved with us at that time, but a check arrived for $1,100.

One day I received a phone call from someone who heard about what we were doing and wanted to send regular financial support. The person's pledge completed the amount of money we needed for Jack's monthly salary. Just as I got off the phone, Jack pulled into our driveway.

I asked, "Jack, what did it cost for you to move?"

He said, "Well, Henry, as best I can tell, it cost me $1,100."

We took a step of faith by believing that the God who knows where we are is the God who can touch people anywhere and cause them to know where we are and what we need. We made the adjustments and were obedient. We believed that the God who called Jack also said, "I AM Provider." As we obeyed, God demonstrated Himself to be our Provider. In an extremely practical way, that experience led us into a deeper love relationship with our all-sufficient God.

God Reveals Himself

Sometimes God tries to get our attention by revealing where He is at work. We see it, but we do not immediately identify it as His activity. We say to ourselves, "I don't know whether or not God wants me to get involved here. I had better pray about it." By the time we pray, the opportunity to join God is gone. A tender, sensitive heart will be ready to respond to God at the slightest prompting. God makes your heart tender and sensitive in the love relationship so you are in tune with what is on His heart for the circumstances around you.

If you are going to join God in His work, you need to know where He is working. The Scriptures identify things only God can do. You need to learn to identify these. Then when something happens around you that only God can do, you will recognize it as God's activity. This does not deny God's initiative. Unless God opens your spiritual eyes, you will not know He is the One at work. He takes the initiative to open your eyes.

Are You Available to God?

Jim worked hard to become the CEO of his company. For years he had focused on climbing the corporate ladder, paying whatever price was necessary to get to the top. Jim had never asked God why He had placed him in his influential position. Jim prayed and asked God to open his eyes to what He was doing in the company. That week someone on his staff began talking about the Bible. When Jim answered the questions, the employee asked him how he knew so much about the Bible. He asked Jim what he could do to know the Bible the way Jim did.

Pray and watch to see what God does next. Only the Father knows what He has purposed, and He knows the best way to accomplish His will. He knows why He brought these individuals together in this company and why He gave Jim the responsibility of bringing them together. After you pray, get off your knees and watch to see what God does next.

For Jim, it might be to lead a Bible study for interested employees on Wednesdays during the lunch hour. Suppose someone in the plant comes to Jim and says, "My family is really having a hard time financially. I am having an especially tough time with my teenager."

Make the connection.
Jim would pray, "God, show me where You are at work." He needs to make the connection between his prayers and what happens next. If you do not connect what happens next, you may miss God's answer to your prayer. Always connect what happens next. So, then what should Jim do next?

Find out what God is already doing by asking probing questions.
Ask the kind of questions that will reveal what is happening in a person's life to find out what God is doing.

The person responds, "I really don't have a relationship with God. But since having this problem with my teenager, I sure have been thinking about it." Or "When I was a kid, I used to go to Sunday School. My mom and dad made me go. I got away from it, but our financial problems have really caused me to think about this." Those statements sound as if God is at work in the person's life. He may be drawing the person to Himself, causing the person to seek God, or bringing conviction of sin.

God Invites You

When you want to know what God is doing around you, pray. Watch to see what happens next. Make the connection between your prayer and what follows. Find out what God is doing by asking probing questions. Then listen. Be ready to make the adjustments required to join God in what He is already doing.

Frequently, the reason we do not join God is because we are not committed to join Him. We want God to bless us, not to work through us. Do not look for ways God is going to bless you. Look for ways God is going to reveal Himself by working through you and beyond you to accomplish His purposes. God's work in you will bring a blessing to you and others, but the blessing is a by-product of your obedience and experience of God at work in your midst.

TRUTH 4:
GOD SPEAKS TO YOU

When God Speaks, Respond

Scripture shows that when God reveals to you what He is doing, that is the time to respond. Although the completion of God's work may be a long time away—for example, Abraham's son was born 25 years after God's promise—the time God comes to you is the moment for your response. That is when you need to adjust your life to Him. You may need to prepare for what He is going to do through you.

What God initiates, He completes. Isaiah confirmed this truth when God said:

"What I have said, that will I bring about; what I have planned, that will I do" (Isaiah 46:11).

Earlier he warned God's people,

"The Lord Almighty has sworn, 'Surely, as I have planned, so it will be, and as I have purposed, so it will stand.'

For the Lord Almighty has purposed, and who can thwart him? His hand is stretched out, and who can turn it back?" (Isaiah 14:24,27).

God says that if He lets His people know what He is about to do, it is as good as done—He Himself will bring it to pass (also see 1 Kings 8:56; Philippians 1:6).

This holds enormous implications for individual believers, churches, and denominations. When we come to God to know what He is about to do where we are, we also have the assurance that what God indicates He is about to do will certainly occur.

The Power of Prayer

I met a wonderful African-American missionary serving in Zambia. He told me of the millions of AIDS orphans in Africa and of the terrible suffering they endured. He shared his burden for African-American churches in the United States to minister to this enormous need. As the missionary shared, the Holy Spirit impressed on me that I was to be a part of God's activity for this need. I told the missionary that I was deeply moved by what he had said and that I would be glad to help in any way I could. I explained that I did not have many contacts in African-American churches. Nevertheless, I would be praying, and I would respond to whatever God directed me to do next.

I had been home for about two days when the phone rang. The call was from one of the leading African-American pastors in the US. He said he was hosting one of the largest gatherings of African-American church leaders and wanted me to speak to them. I recognized that God was giving me my next instructions.

Not long after that, I received another unusual invitation. This time it was to speak to a group of ambassadors from Africa at the United Nations. After I shared with them about being spiritual leaders in their homelands, they gave me their business cards and asked me to visit their countries. Since that time, God has steadily revealed to me His great love for the people of Africa and for the millions of people who suffer there daily. Every conversation with God has limitless possibilities attached to it, because He "is able to do immeasurably more than all we ask or imagine, according to his power that is at work within us" (Ephesians 3:20).

God Speaks in Different Ways

A critical requirement for understanding and experiencing God is to clearly know when He is speaking. If Christians do not know when God is speaking, then they are in trouble at the heart of their Christian lives. God speaks to us in these ways:

· God speaks through the Holy Spirit to reveal Himself, His purposes, and His ways.

· God speaks through the Bible.

· God speaks through prayer.

· God speaks through circumstances.

· God speaks through the church and believers.

A Wrong Pattern

I hear many people say something like this: "Lord, I really want to know Your will. Stop me if I am wrong and bless me if I am right" or "Lord, I will proceed in this direction. Close the door if it is not Your will." This approach isn't found in Scripture.

Don't let experience alone guide your life. Don't allow yourself to be led merely by tradition, methods, or formulas. Often people trust these because they appear easier than cultivating an intimate walk with God. People do as they please and put the whole burden of responsibility on God. If they are wrong, He must intervene and stop them. If they make a mistake, they blame Him. God is not obligated to stop you from making a mistake!

If you want to know the will and voice of God, you must devote time and effort to cultivate a love relationship with Him. That is what He wants!

A Lawyer Learns to Hear God's Voice

God has given me a wonderful opportunity to lead a Bible study for several hundred men and women in the workplace. We meet monthly from 6:30 to 7:30 a.m. One lawyer drives nearly every month from Macon to south Atlanta. I became his friend and followed his deep desire to know God's clear will, especially in cases he was handling. He had a very sensitive case involving a prisoner who was incarcerated for life. She became a Christian and desired to gain parole so she could help others know Christ as she knew Him. It seemed impossible, but the more the lawyer learned how God guides His children, the more he trusted God and obeyed what He told him to do. After a long period of time, his client was not only paroled but also remarried the father of her 11-year-old son, and they are living happily and faithfully to this day. The Christian lawyer rejoices that he knows how and when God speaks and what happens when he obeys.

Please Cancel My Request!

Have you ever prayed for one thing and received another? I have. When that used to happen to me, some dear soul would inevitably say, "God is trying to get you to persist. Keep praying until you receive what you are asking for."

I kept asking God for one thing, but I kept receiving something else. During one of these experiences I started reading from Mark 2, which tells the account of the four men who brought their crippled friend to Jesus to be healed. Because of the large crowd they opened a hole in the roof of the house and let the man down in front of Jesus. Jesus said, "Son, your sins are forgiven" (Mark 2:5).

I started to read on, but I sensed the Spirit of God saying, "Henry, did you see that?" I went back and meditated on that Scripture. Under the Holy Spirit's guiding, I discovered a wonderful truth: the four men asked Jesus to physically heal the man, but Jesus forgave the man's sins. They asked for one thing, and Jesus gave another! This man and his friends asked for a temporary gift, but Jesus wanted to make the man a child of God for eternity so he could inherit everything!

I found myself weeping before God and saying, "O God, if I ever ask You for one thing and You have more to give me than I am asking, please cancel my request!"

TRUTH 5:
YOUR CRISIS
OF BELIEF

What Do You Believe About God?

The word *crisis* comes from a Greek word that means *decision* or *judgment*. A crisis of belief is not a calamity in your life but a turning point where you must make a decision. You must decide what you truly believe about God. The way you respond at this turning point will determine whether you become involved with God in something God-sized that only He can do or whether you continue to go your own way and miss what He has purposed for your life. This is not a one-time experience. It is a regular occurrence. The way you live your life is a testimony of what you believe about God.

When God invites you to join Him in His work, He has a God-sized assignment for you. You will quickly realize you cannot do what He is asking on your own. If God doesn't help you, you will fail. This is the crisis of belief—when you must decide whether or not to believe God for what He wants to do through you. At this point, many people decide not to follow what they sense God is leading them to do. Then they wonder why they do not experience God's presence and activity the way other Christians do.

Walking by Faith

One year the members of our finance committee said, "Pastor, you have taught us to walk by faith in every area in the life of our church except the budget." I asked them to explain. They said, "We develop the budget on the basis of what we believe we can do. It does not reflect that we expect God to do anything."

"Then how do you feel we ought to produce the budget?" I asked.

They said, "First, we ought to determine all God wants to do through us in the coming year. Second, we need to estimate what that will cost. Then we need to divide the budget revenue into three categories:

1. What we plan to do through our own giving.

2. What others have promised to do to help.

3. What we must depend on God to do."

As a church, we prayed and decided God wanted us to use this approach to budgeting. We did not try to dream our own dreams for God. We had to be absolutely sure God was leading us to do the things we put in the budget. Then we listed what that would cost. We estimated what we thought our people would give and what others (the mission board, partnership churches, and individuals) had said they would contribute. The difference between what we could reasonably expect to receive and the total was what we asked God to provide.

A Crisis of Belief

The big question was what our operating budget would be. By faith, we adopted the grand total as our operating budget. At this point, we reached a crisis of belief. Did we really believe the God who had led us to do these things would provide the resources to bring them to pass? Anytime God leads you to do something that has God-sized dimensions, you will face a crisis of belief. At that point what you do next reveals what you believe about God.

That year we set our budget at more than twice the amount we would normally have planned. Yet, at year-end, God had exceeded even that amount by providing us with revenue we could not have anticipated. God taught our church a lesson in faith that radically changed us all.

It's a Challenge

By the time he was in the sixth grade, he had discovered marijuana, organized a gang, and was dealing drugs. He went to jail for the first time when he was 11. At age 19—miserable, addicted to drugs, sick of the life he was living—Fernando Hernandez gave his life to Christ. He readily admits that it has been a challenge to serve God in the years since. He also says, "If God is in the deal, stay in it."

"Staying in the deal" led Fernando to start a gang-prevention ministry called "It's A Challenge." His life story gave his witness credibility with at-risk teenagers. "I was right where they are. Thank God, Jesus found me."

He started It's A Challenge to focus on bringing typically hard-to-reach students together for prayer, Bible study, and encouragement at before-school meetings. There they found people who cared and a gospel witness as well as reasons to stay drug-free, in school, and out of gangs. He said:

"Some of the kids who came might not do homework. They might not read very well. But we would take one day's lesson [of *Experiencing God*] each week. That study turned into a yearlong Bible school. The kids committed to the work and they kept coming back. The experience had a good effect on their schoolwork and their hearts."

The message of this ministry continues to be that students have choices and hope. And, if they trust God, He will change and use their lives.

God Put Confidence in My Heart

God is far more concerned with your walking with Him than He is interested in getting a job done for Him. When the world sees things happening through God's people that cannot be explained except that God Himself has done them, the world will be drawn to such a God.

Our church in Saskatoon was growing and needed more space. We sensed God leading us to enlarge our facility even though we had only $749 in the building fund. The building was going to cost $220,000. We didn't have the foggiest notion how to do it.

We did much of the work to save labor costs. Still, halfway through the building program we were $100,000 short. Those dear people looked to their pastor to see if I believed God would accomplish what He called us to. God put confidence in my heart that the God who was leading us would show us how to do it.

God began providing the necessary funds, but we were still $60,000 short toward the end. We had expected money from a Texas foundation. Delay after delay occurred that we could not understand. Then, one day for just two hours the currency-exchange rate for the Canadian dollar hit the lowest point in history. That was exactly the time the Texas foundation wired the money to Canada. That gave us $60,000 more than we would have received otherwise.

Actions Speak

When God invites you to join Him and you face a crisis of belief, what you do next reveals what you believe about God. Your actions speak louder than your words. James 2:26 says, "As the body without the spirit is dead, so faith without deeds is dead." When you face a crisis of belief, what you do demonstrates what you believe. Faith without action is dead! Genuine faith is demonstrated by action.

Outward appearances of success do not always indicate faith, and outward appearances of failure do not always reflect a lack of faith. A faithful servant is one who does what his Master tells him, whatever the outcome may be. Consider Jesus: He endured the cross, but now He is seated next to the throne of God! What a reward for faithfulness! Don't grow weary in being faithful. A reward awaits faithful servants.

TRUTH 6:
YOU MUST ADJUST YOUR LIFE

A Young Couple's Sacrifice

When a need arose in one of our mission churches 40 miles away, I asked the church to pray that God would call someone to move to that community to serve as the lay pastor of the mission. A young couple responded. Because the husband was attending university, they had very little money.

If they took up residence in the mission community, he would have to commute 80 miles a day to the university. I knew they couldn't afford to do it. I said, "No, I can't let you do that" and named several reasons why that would not be fair.

This young couple was deeply grateful that God had saved them. The young man looked at me and said, "Pastor, don't deny me the opportunity to sacrifice for my Lord." That statement crushed me. How could I refuse? Yet, I knew this couple would have to pay a high price because our church had been obedient to start new missions.

We had prayed for God to call a lay pastor, so I needed to be open to God's answering our prayers in an unexpected way. When this couple responded with a deep sense of commitment and personal sacrifice, our church affirmed their sense of call, and God provided for their needs!

Absolute Surrender

God frequently requires adjustments in areas of your life that you have never considered or been open to in the past. You may have heard someone say something like this: "Don't ever tell God something you don't want to do. ...

That is what He will ask you to do." God is not looking for ways to make your life difficult. However, He intends to be the Lord of your life. When you identify a place where you refuse to allow His lordship, that is where He will go to work. He is seeking **absolute surrender**. God may or may not require you to do the thing you identified, but He will keep working until you are willing for Him to be Lord of all. Remember, because God loves you, His will is always best! Any adjustment God expects you to make is for your good. As you follow Him, the time may come when your life and future may depend on your adjusting quickly to God's directives.

You don't adjust your life to a concept. You align your life to God. You alter your viewpoints to resemble His. You change your ways to be like His ways. After you make the necessary adjustments, He will tell you what to do next in order to obey Him. When you follow Him, you will experience Him doing through you something only He can do.

Obedience Is Costly

Hudson Taylor, a great man of prayer and faith, responded to God's call to go to China in the 19th century as a missionary. Obeying God meant leaving his widowed mother alone. By the end of Hudson's life in 1905, he had been used by God to found the China Inland Mission. There were 205 preaching stations, 849 missionaries, and 125,000 Chinese Christians—a testimony of a life absolutely surrendered to God. Hudson Taylor described something of the cost he and his mother experienced as he obeyed God's will to go to China:

"My beloved, now sainted, mother had come to see me off from Liverpool. Never shall I forget that day, nor how she went with me into the little cabin that was to be my home for nearly six long months. With a mother's loving hand she smoothed the little bed. She sat by my side, and joined me in the last hymn that we should sing together before the long parting.

We knelt down, and she prayed—the last mother's prayer I was to hear before starting for China. Then notice was given that we must separate, and we had to say good-bye, never expecting to meet on earth again.

For my sake she restrained her feelings as much as possible. We parted; and she went on shore, giving me her blessing! I stood alone on deck, and she followed the ship as we moved towards the dock gates. As we passed through the gates, and the separation really commenced, I shall never forget the cry of anguish wrung from that mother's heart. It went through me like a knife. I never knew so fully, until then, what 'God so loved the world' meant. And I am quite sure that my precious mother learned more of the love of God to the perishing in that hour than in all her life before."

Leaving home and family on a dangerous mission was a costly step for Hudson Taylor to take. His mother loved the Lord so much she was willing to pay the price of releasing her son to missions. Both of the Taylors had to pay a high cost for obedience. Yet they both experienced God's love in a way they had never known before.

Without God, You Can Do Nothing

Once a church asked, "O God, how do You want to reach our community through us and build a great church?" God led them to start a bus ministry and provide transportation for children and adults to come to church. They did what God told them to do, and their church grew into a great church.

They were flattered when people from all over the country began to ask, "What are you doing to grow so rapidly?" They wrote a book on how to build great churches through a bus ministry. Thousands of churches began to buy buses to reach their communities, believing the method was the key to growth. Later many sold the buses, saying, "It didn't work for us."

It never works. He works! The method is never the key to accomplishing God's purposes. The key is your relationship with the Person of God. When you want to know how God wants you to reach your city, start a new church, or be involved in His work, ask Him. Then when He tells you, don't be surprised if you can't find any church that is doing it that same way. Why? God wants you to know Him. If you follow someone else's plan, use a method, or emphasize a program, you tend to forget about your dependence on God. You leave the relationship with God and go after a method or a program. That is spiritual adultery.

Without God at work in you, you can do nothing to produce Kingdom fruit. When God purposes to do something, He guarantees it will come to pass. He is the One who will accomplish what He intends to do. If you depend on anything other than God, you are asking for failure in Kingdom terms.

NOTES

TRUTH 7:
YOU CAN
EXPERIENCE GOD

Obedience Provided
Future Blessing

We were still an extremely small church, and we were trying to staff and support three mission churches. We were asked to sponsor another mission in Winnipeg, Manitoba—510 miles from our church. Someone would have to drive this 1,020-mile round trip in order to meet with the people in the mission. At first glance this sounded like an impossible task for our little group.

I shared with our congregation that a faithful group of people had been meeting for more than two years and wanted to start a church. They had approached us to sponsor them.

We had to determine whether this was God's work and whether He was revealing His activity to us. Was this our invitation to join Him in what He was doing? The church agreed this was God's invitation, and we knew we had to obey. We agreed to sponsor the new mission. Then we asked God to show us how and to give us strength and resources to do it.

A number of times I drove to Winnipeg to preach and minister to the people. Sooner than we saw Him provide for any of our other mission churches, God provided a pastor and a salary for Winnipeg. However, the story of our obedience did not end there. That original church became the mother church to many other mission churches and started an entire association of churches.

When our oldest son, Richard, finished seminary, this church in Winnipeg called him to be its pastor. A year later, the church called our second son Tom to be the associate pastor. Little did I know that this one act of obedience, which at first appeared impossible, held such potential for future blessing for my family.

Wait on the Lord

Grass that is here today and gone tomorrow does not require much time to mature. A big oak tree that lives for generations requires much more time to develop. God is concerned about your life through eternity. Allow Him to take all the time He wants to shape you for His purposes. Larger assignments require longer periods of preparation.

Let God orient you to Himself. The servant does not tell the Master what kind of task he wants. The servant waits on his Master for the assignment. Be patient. Waiting on the Lord should not be idle time. Let God use waiting times to mold and shape your character. Let God use those times to purify your life and make you a clean vessel for His service.

As you obey Him, God will prepare you for the assignment that is suitable for you. Any task, however, that comes from the Maker of the universe is important. Don't use human standards to measure the importance or value of the task God gives.

When You Obey but Doors Close, Then What?

Suppose you sense God's call to a task, a place, or an assignment. You set about to do it, but everything goes wrong. Often people say, "I guess that was not God's will."

God calls you into a relationship with Himself. Be careful how you interpret circumstances. Many times we jump to a conclusion too quickly. God is moving us in one direction to tell us what He is about to do. We immediately jump to our own conclusion about what He is doing because our reasoning sounds logical. We start following the logic of our own thinking, and then nothing seems to work out. We tend to ignore our relationship with God and take matters into our own hands. Don't do that!

Most of the time when God calls you or gives you a direction, He is not calling you to do something for Him. He is telling you what He is about to do where you are.

God's Plan

Does God plan your life for eternity and then turn you loose to work out His intentions? God's desire is for a relationship. We get in trouble when we try to get God to tell us if He wants us to be a Christian businessperson, music director, schoolteacher, preacher, or missionary. We want to know if He wants us to serve in our home country or go to Japan or Canada. God doesn't usually give you a one-time assignment and leave you there forever. Yes, you may be placed in one job in one place for an extended period, but God's assignments come to you on a daily basis.

God calls you to a relationship in which He is Lord—in which you are willing to do and be anything He chooses. If you recognize and follow Him as Lord, He may lead you to do and be things you would never have dreamed of. If you don't, you may lock yourself into a job or an assignment and miss something God wants to do through you.

I've heard people say things like "God called me to be a _____, so this other thing couldn't possibly be His will." Or "My spiritual gift is _____, so this ministry couldn't be God's will for me."

Spiritual Gifts

God will never give you an assignment He will not enable you to complete. *That is what a spiritual gift is—a supernatural empowering to accomplish the assignment God gives you.* Don't focus on your talents, abilities, and interests in determining God's will. I have heard many people say, "I would really like to do that; therefore, it must be God's will."

That kind of response is self-centered. Instead, become God-centered. God is Lord, and your response should be something like: "Lord, I will do anything Your Kingdom requires of me. Wherever You want me to go, I'll go. Whatever the circumstances, I'm willing to follow. If You want to meet a need through my life, I am Your servant, and I will do whatever is required."

Spiritual Markers

I have found it helpful to identify spiritual markers in my life. Each time I have encountered God's call or directions for my life, I have mentally built a spiritual marker at that point. A spiritual marker identifies a time of transition, decision, or direction when I clearly know God has guided me. Over time I can look back at these spiritual markers and see how God has faithfully directed my life according to His divine purpose.

When I face a decision about God's direction, I review those spiritual markers. I don't take the next step without the context of God's full activity in my life. This helps me see God's perspective for my past and present. Then I examine the options before me, looking to see which direction is most consistent with what God has been doing in my life. Often one of these opportunities will be right in line with what God has already been doing.

If none of the directions seem consistent, I continue to pray and wait on the Lord's guidance. When circumstances do not align with what God is saying in the Bible and in prayer, I assume the timing may be wrong. Then, I wait for God to reveal His timing.

When We Are Weak, God Is Strong

Years ago, my wife Marilynn nearly died of an illness. God had called me to start a church mission in another town. Marilynn had not yet fully recovered. I felt helpless and broken from the ordeal. We had five children at home. Each time I had to leave, I would call Marilynn to tell her I loved her. This time, Marilynn was crying. "Henry, I just can't take it anymore," she said. "It's just so hard. I want you to be here, but I know you are doing what God wants you to do. I'm at the end of my rope and don't know what to do."

I went home, and together we lifted our faces heavenward and prayed, "Oh God, we are doing all we know to do. There is just no strength left." Suddenly, there came over us an incredible presence and power of God. I don't think I ever knew the power of Christ until I came to the point of desperation.

From nothing, I learned everything. Only when we were weakest could we begin to realize God's awesome power.

Once more, we experienced God. So can you.

Notes

MOST BIBLE STUDIES HELP PEOPLE.

THIS ONE CHANGES THEM FOREVER.

Actually, God changes people. But for more than 16 years, He's used *Experiencing God* to help. This study will show you how to know God intimately and encourage you to step out in faith and join Him in His work — with miraculous results. The newly revised study contains many examples: from Angola Prison inmates earning seminary degrees to the spiritual and economic rebirth of a poor Appalachian community. These testimonies are truly amazing, but God has more to do and He has a vital role just for you! Will you join Him? Order your study online, call 1.800.458.2772, or visit the LifeWay Christian Store serving you.

WWW.LIFEWAY.COM/EG

About the Authors

Henry T. Blackaby is the primary author of *Experiencing God* and founder of Blackaby Ministries International. He has served as pastor of churches in the US and Canada, spoken in more than 200 countries, and written more than a dozen books. He and his wife Marilynn have five children, all of whom serve with their families in ministry.

Claude V. King is an editor in chief at LifeWay Christian Resources. He wrote the learning activities for *Experiencing God*, has authored or coauthored over 20 books, and serves as president of the board of directors for Final Command Ministry.

Richard Blackaby is Henry's oldest son and is current president of Blackaby Ministries International. He has served as a pastor and seminary president. Richard contributed materials to the revised edition of *Experiencing God*. He is author of *Crosseekers*, *Putting a Face on Grace*, and *Unlimiting God*, and coauthor of a dozen books with his father.